OFFICE HOURS

What Every University Student Needs to Know

Robyn Brinks Lockwood

University of Michigan Press
Ann Arbor

ISBN-13: 978-0-472-03760-5 (print)
ISBN-13: 978-0-472-12630-9 (ebook)

2022   2021   2020   2019   4   3   2   1

■ Acknowledgments

I would like to thank my editor, Kelly Sippell, for her valuable input during the development of this book and her dedication to producing materials that can help instructors be even better at what they do in the classroom. Many thanks to all my students at Stanford University who worked diligently and with great participation. Concerns students shared with me about office hours during my own office hours led to this book. I wanted to make their academic lives less stressful. Thanks, as always, to my parents, both former teachers, for their encouragement to do what is best for the students, and my husband, a former engineering professor, whose stories about his own students' needs in his department helped me better structure my own ESL classroom. And, to my favorite boys: Tim, Darrin, and Nathan…I'm so proud of you all.

We would also like to acknowledge the actors who appear in the videos: Ana Dean, Kelsey Dean, Angie Feak, Christine B. Feak, Scott Ham, Adam Jazairi, Sheryl Leicher, Sun Park, and Karen Pitton.

Thank you to Mosseri Enterprises for video production.

■ Contents

◼ Introduction: Why I Wrote This Book

Having taught for many years at the university level, I thought I could no longer be surprised by what students needed and wanted the most help with. I maintained a checklist of things students need to not just survive—but also thrive—in a post-secondary setting. Of course, my checklist is always evolving.

When I moved to teaching at the university level, I learned that students were not prepared for 50-minute lectures, so I developed textbooks and materials to better prepare them to be true academic listeners (*4 Point: Listening for Academic Purposes,* 2016). I also realized they struggled with communicating in social contexts, many having never been in a setting requiring them to communicate effectively with professors, peers, and colleagues, so I wrote a speaking textbook focusing on this type of language (*Speaking in Social Contexts,* 2018). I also knew that students did not have nearly as large a vocabulary base as they needed because they seemed to know only words from the Academic Word List and/or they had memorized every word on the GRE® vocabulary list; to deal with this I prepared vocabulary strategies (*4 Point: Reading for Academic Purposes,* 2016) to help them. You will study listening, speaking, and vocabulary if you take English classes.

My checklist of topics to cover when teaching university coursework was compiled after teaching countless classes from the beginning of my second language teaching career, holding 12 years' worth of office hours at Stanford University, and having many solicited meetings with students I called on to inform my teaching, course materials development, and textbook writing. I always want to be teaching what students actually want and need to know, and not simply what teachers and writers think students want and need to know. This book is a result of those classes, office hours, and meetings. It is what my students told me they wanted and needed.

There are things you can do to prepare yourself for academic listening, speaking, reading, writing, grammar, and vocabulary. A myriad of published books includes skills, strategies, and practice to help you prepare for the academic classes you will take at a university in a college setting. However, one thing students have discussed with me over and over again is not covered in any textbook—what to do or say during office hours with a professor or TA. A few examples include things like:

- not knowing how to greet the professor (do you use a title, do you use a formal greeting?).
- being unsure which words to use (to ask for advice, seek help, explain an absence).
- not knowing whether or not to sit down.

- not having an idea of how to properly word an email message asking for an appointment or explaining an absence.
- not following the cues professors or TAs were using to indicate the office hour was over and that it was time to leave.
- not being properly prepared to be a TA and manage your own office hours.

My students often shared stories about their interactions with professors/instructors during office hours. These stories struck me because students tended to ask about office hours during my speaking classes or during a meeting with me after a failed or awkward office hour interaction with another professor or TA. The types of office hour visits my students talked about ranged from one-on-one meetings with professors or TAs to going to office hours with other students; they also asked about online office hour interactions, either as an individual or in groups, such as the ever-growing popularity of office hours held via Zoom, course (learning) management systems, or other video services.

I also recognized that students often struggled during office hours with me, and I'm the sympathetic communication instructor who is there to help. One thing I noticed was that my students were not afraid to talk to me, but they were not handling the office hour interaction the "right" way. If they were struggling during a meeting with the ESL instructor, then what was happening when they met with professors in their general education, major, and upper-level graduate classes who were not as sympathetic to the challenges of being a new student at the university level? Those professors expect all students—regardless of what language they speak—to do the same work as everyone else in the class.

An important reason for writing the book was that the challenge of "office hours" is not just for second language speakers. Office hours are a unique speaking event (or genre) for everyone. It's not just students from other countries who speak other languages who struggle with knowing what to do and not to do during an office hour meeting with a TA or professor. **The university office hour interaction is new to everyone who attends a university.** This event is something that all college students need to learn to navigate.

Thinking about how I could help them as a college instructor reminded me of something my mother always told me about taking my vitamins and drinking my orange juice or what my dad always said about going to the dentist when my teeth didn't hurt: You want to do these things to prevent the problems, not do them after you have the problems. When it came to office hours, I wanted all students to be better prepared for an office hour regardless of who it was with. I wanted them to be prepared in advance; I wanted to help them avoid the failed interaction altogether. And I wanted TAs to feel more comfortable and be better at their jobs while also better navigating their own office hours with professors they work for or professors they meet with.

Because many of my students were going to be TAs and were going to be holding their own office hours and because all students would eventually have to attend an office hour in some form or fashion, I decided to start teaching office hours as part of one of my academic speaking classes at the university. I began thinking about the language and structure—yes, structure—of an office hour. I realized that if students realized that office hours followed a certain structure and if they could learn the associated language needed for each part of that structure, they could manage office hours more successfully. Hence, this overview of office hours was born.

This book will teach you what office hours are and how they are used, introduce you to the five parts of an office hour, and present the language you will need for each of those five parts—both as a student using office hours or as a TA holding office hours. I have included some general do's and don'ts to keep in mind as guidelines when preparing for or reflecting on an office hour. Pronunciation notes are offered as well. For current and prospective TAs, boxes titled **Reflections for TAs** pose questions designed to help you manage your job and better serve your students and the professors you work for. Using all these materials should ensure that all participants start, progress through, and end each office hour positively.

I also believe that the language and strategies in this book can extend beyond what you study independently or in a classroom. They can extend beyond what you read or experience in campus office hours and be applied to professional contexts, such as meetings with bosses and colleagues, or in a variety of other contexts such as appointments, seminars, conferences, or business/social dinners/ events.

Four video clips (available for free online) accompany this book (www.press.umich.edu/elt/compsite/officehours). Two video analysis tasks are integrated into the chapters, and two appear at the end of the book as capstones. Transcripts and analysis questions are included in the book.

1

What Are Office Hours?

Defining *office hours* might not be as easy as dictionaries or professors make it seem. Merriam Webster lists three definitions: (1) the time during the day that people work in an office, (2) the time during the day when an instructor is available to meet with students in his or her office, and (3) a time during the day when people can see a doctor or dentist. Obviously, the second definition is the one we want, and using this definition does make understanding office hours seem easy for everyone on a college campus: **Office hours are the time that professors or instructors are in their offices and available for students to meet with them.** Basically, they are meetings that are common in college and university settings.

Professors and instructors at the college level are obligated to set aside time to be available to students in their office; that's where the term *office hours* comes from. Universities have different requirements for how many hours professors and instructors need to be available; for example, professors/instructors might have to offer two hours of office hours for every class they teach.

An important thing for students to keep in mind is that if a professor is not teaching, it does not mean that he or she is in the office waiting for students to visit. Rather, each professor/instructor chooses certain hours on certain days to be available for students; these hours are "posted" by the office but are more commonly listed on the course syllabus. Examples of the hours a professor might be available for students to visit are Mondays and Wednesdays from 10 AM to 12 PM or Tuesdays from 1 PM to 3 PM. There are some rules about when and how to "go" to office hours (see pages 20–21), but generally students need to find out when their professors' office hours are before going to the office. You are always welcome to go without doing that, but if you do not have an appointment and you are visiting during a time that it is not posted as an office hour, there is no guarantee that the professor will be able to see you even if he or she is there.

The Purpose and Goals of an Office Hour

Students visit office hours and professors hold office hours to achieve the same general purpose: exchange of information. The two parties—the student and the professor—are discussing or sharing information. What they are sharing information about might vary; for example, they might be discussing the student's performance, content from the class, planning for the next term, or research or graduate school opportunities. Regardless of topic, the goal is to make sure both parties have all the information they need and agree on a solution or plan before the end of the meeting.

Some common reasons for an office hour meeting are:

- to ask for a reference letter.
- to ask questions or make comments you were unable to or were hesitant to ask in class.
- to explain why you missed class.
- to get more information about upcoming classes, lectures, or assignments.
- to get professional (career) advice.
- to help yourself stand out from others, especially in large classes with hundreds or thousands of students.
- to learn more about the professor or course.
- to receive feedback about your work, a grade, or an assignment.
- to seek general advice.
- to talk about graduate school, becoming a TA, or other courses in the program or that the professor teaches.

Keep in mind that this is not an all-inclusive list. Students can schedule office hours for practically any reason. Some other reasons that students might visit a professor include discussing time management struggles, discussing campus or personal issues that may be affecting a student's emotional or physical well-being, or meeting to talk about the course content or get extra practice using a language.

The course syllabus, which is your guide to what is expected of you during the course, includes a lot of information. While there is no set format for a course syllabus, it often includes course policies (such as plagiarism or attendance), required textbooks or materials, a schedule of assignments, a list of course objectives, and information about office hours. Make sure to read the syllabus or check the course website to learn when (available times) and where (the professor or TA's office number/location) to meet for office hours and the expectations for those office hours.

TASK ONE

Read the list of common reasons for having an office hour meeting and think about (1) which of them are reasons you are familiar with and (2) which of them are reasons that you might go to visit a professor/instructor during office hours.

_____ to ask for a reference letter

_____ to ask questions or make comments you were unable to / were hesitant to ask in class

_____ to explain why you missed class

_____ to get more information about upcoming classes, lectures, or assignments

_____ to get professional (career) advice

_____ to help yourself stand out from others, especially in large classes with hundreds or thousands of students

_____ to learn more about the professor or course

_____ to receive feedback about your work, a grade, or an assignment

_____ to seek general advice

_____ to talk about graduate school, becoming a TA, or other courses

Who Can You Meet with During an Office Hour Meeting?

You might assume that you will meet directly with professors during office hours, but that is not necessarily true. For large courses, many professors have TAs to help them meet with students since they cannot possibly meet with everyone. Small courses might also have TAs that are hired to help you with questions about the course content while the professor handles other topics during an office hour. You may also be surprised to learn that an office hour might not be private; in other words, a TA's office hours might be "open," which means that other students from the class or another section of the class can come and go throughout that time period to get help with the work.

The Teaching Assistant

A teaching assistant (TA) is most often a graduate student who has been hired by the professor or department to help with the teaching responsibilities for a course you are enrolled in. In some ways, what happens during an office hour visit with a TA simplifies the experience (as opposed to a professor, which is discussed later). The first thing to note is that office hours with your professor may be very different from those of a TA. A TA's office hours are usually designed specifically to help students with whatever current assignments they are working on for class. This situation is especially true for large, first-year courses with hundreds of students enrolled, such as Psychology 101 or Introduction to

Political Science, or for especially difficult classes, such as second- or third-year classes that are more focused on content or for students majoring in that field.

Other reasons to visit a TA's office hours, besides getting help with an assignment, are:

- to ask questions or make comments you were unable to or were hesitant to ask in class.
- to get more information about upcoming classes, lectures, or assignments.
- to help yourself stand out from others, especially in large classes with hundreds or thousands of students (TAs keep attendance and let the professors know who visited their office hours).
- to learn more about the professor or course.
- to meet other students in the course (and potentially form study groups or make friends because many TA office hours are not individual meetings).
- to receive feedback about your work (TAs likely took the course themselves in years past).
- to talk about graduate school, becoming a TA, or other courses (get advice on which courses and which professors to take).

TASK TWO

1. Are there any items on the list that you feel are irrelevant? Why?

2. Are there any other reasons you can think of to visit a TA's office hours?

3. Does this task change your ideas about TAs or the office hours of TAs?

Reflections for TAs

1. If you are already a TA, how does this list compare to what your professor or department tasked you to do? If you are not a TA yet, ask if your department has a list and then compare it to this list.

2. Which of these do you like/would you like best? Why? Include any additional items your professor or department has asked you to do.

3. Which of these are/seem most challenging? Why? Include any additional items your professor or department has asked you to do.

4. Which of these do you/would you want to prepare better for? For the item you select, write a short role-play dialogue in which a student comes to your office hours.

The Professor

The reasons for visiting a professor's office hours vary more widely than those for TAs. Sometimes you may simply want to begin building a bond with a professor whose class you are taking or with whom you hope to work—perhaps you just admire this professor and are looking for a mentor or maybe this is a person whose lab or research group you hope to join, especially if you are a graduate student pursuing a Master's or PhD degree. You may also want to meet with a former professor during their office hours. Many professors like when former students visit and update them on their courses, projects, or careers.

You may want to use a professor's office hours if you:

- already visited a TA assigned to the course.
- are not required to only visit the TA.
- have a TA who is not also the instructor (if the TA is also teaching, you should visit their office hours).
- missed class.
- don't understand the material.
- need clarification of content.
- want feedback on a grade or assignment.
- want professional (career) advice.
- want course advice (what courses should you take next).
- need general advice.
- are majoring in the field of study or enrolled in a higher-level course (as opposed to a first-year course).

- need a reference letter.
- want to work with the professor's lab or research group or discuss other research or internship opportunities.
- are a former student.

TASK THREE

1. Are there any items on the list that you feel are not something you would talk to your professor about? What items on the list might you talk to a professor of a first-year, 100-level, undergraduate course you are taking? What items on the list might you talk to a professor about if you are taking an upper-level course? What about if you are a graduate student?

2. Are there any other reasons you can think of to visit a professor's office hours?

3. Does this task change your ideas about a professor's office hours?

Reflections for TAs

1. Do you feel any of the items on this list could also be handled by a TA?

2. Which of these do you like/would you like to do for your professor or department? Why?

3. Which of these are/seem most challenging for a TA? Why?

4. Imagine a student asks you about one of the items for which you think they should attend the professor's office hours. For the item you select, write a short role-play dialogue including their request and your response.

TASK FOUR

Some things you can say when you visit a professor's office hours are listed. Rank them from most to least appropriate.

_____ Hi. I'm a student in your 10 AM computer science class. Is this a good time for me to ask some questions about class or should I schedule an appointment with you for another time?

_____ I'm afraid I didn't understand the math problem you had on the board. Can I show you my notes and ask you to talk through the problem with me?

_____ I am not actually taking any of your classes, but I read an article you wrote, and I'm interested in learning more about that topic.

_____ I came by to ask about your research. What is it you like about this particular research field?

_____ I read an article about a topic you covered in class the other day. I was wondering if you're familiar with this article and what your thoughts were on it.

_____ In Monday's class, you said you didn't have time to get into the finer details about [X topic]. Can you maybe tell me a little more about those details now?

_____ I'd like to know more about the topic we discussed in class. Do you have any readings you recommend?

_____ I was hoping you could re-explain the concept we talked about in class. I'm not sure I understand it.

How to Plan an Office Hour Meeting

Drop In

Sometimes a class—for example, your Computer Science 101 course—will have its own specific set of office hours dedicated to anyone enrolled in that particular course, similar to the office hours of TAs. It is also just as likely that the professor's posted office hours will be open to any student of the professor's, including students who are not enrolled in any of the professor's classes this semester/term. Professors typically determine at the beginning of a term what their office hours will be. For example, a professor might have office hours from 10 AM to 12 PM on Mondays and Wednesdays. Some may have different office hours every week, and you may need to check the course website or Canvas or another course management system to find out when office hours are at any given time during the term. Generally, you can think of the office hours as a time when you can *drop in*, or come by at any point during that period of time without an appointment. Office hours might also be posted on the professor's door, listed online, or available from the department administrative assistant.

Make an Appointment

Some professors only have office hours only *by appointment*, which means you need to schedule a meeting with that professor in advance. Actually, many professors, even those with firm office hours, prefer to schedule specific times to meet with students, especially if you have a topic or question that you feel might require a lengthy response or more of the professor's time, like when getting advice about graduate school or a job. Appointments can be scheduled in person (maybe even during drop-in office hours), via email, or by using the scheduler or calendar settings in a course management system such as Canvas. You should be aware that professors do not like no-shows or last-minute cancellations. They have set aside time and arranged to meet with you. If you must cancel, give as much notice as possible and recognize that it may take time to arrange for a rescheduled appointment. Sometimes, professors allow appointments to be made beyond the designated posted office hours.

If a professor only allows visits by appointment and you need more immediate assistance, you should consult with the TA if the course has one, talk with peers taking the course, or talk to other students who have taken the class in the past. Bear in mind that professors usually respond, but they may not respond as quickly as you hope. Professors work with many other students students, attend faculty and administrative meetings, go to conferences, and serve on committees, among many other tasks—all of which can keep them away from their email.

TASK FIVE

Many universities, departments, or offices post information about office hours online. Conduct an online search for a college or university you attend, will attend, or hope to attend. Then answer the questions.

1. What school did you choose to learn more about?

2. What, if any, general information can you find about office hours at your selected school?

Find a professor in a department of interest to you at the school you are researching.

3. Where is that professor's office?

4. What are his or her office hours this term?

5. How do you make an office hour appointment or are all the office hours drop in?

6. Is there a TA for a course you are interested in? What are those office hours?

7. If you had the opportunity to visit during office hours, what is one thing you would want to ask this professor?

Deciding Whether to Go to Office Hours or Send an Email Message

It's important not to misuse (or overuse) office hours. In general, you don't want to use office hour appointments for trivial matters like asking if you need to bring the textbook to class. You certainly don't want to use that time to ask for inappropriate things, such as asking for the professor's lecture notes (you should have taken notes or asked a classmate) or asking the professor to review a draft of your assignment (that is unfair to the professor and to your classmates). Sometimes you might need information that can be handled with a simple email message to the professor. Just be careful! You don't want to ask a question that is answered on the syllabus, on the course website, or in other course materials. For example, don't ask about which chapter to read when or how many pages your paper should be if the syllabus or website lists this information.

Similarly, you need to think about when to send an email message versus when to get the information in a face-to-face meeting. For example, you should not send an email about your grade. Any discussion about grades should be handled during an office hours meeting. Sensitive or personal information should also be handled in person. If you have a concern or are frustrated with something regarding your class, it is best to discuss it in person because it would likely result in long strings of email messages that probably wouldn't solve the problem.

When you email a professor to request an appointment or to manage simple requests for which an office hour is not required, consider following email etiquette, including:

- using your university or school email account (not a personal account)
- stating clearly at the beginning which class you are in
- explaining why you are emailing
- being concise (if an email is very long, maybe it should be an office hour visit)
- using formal wording, tone, and style
- avoiding slang or using all capital letters, emoticons, and other informalities
- using good paragraphing and letter writing format and including a salutation and signature line
- using formal titles (or Professor if they are not a Dr.)
- using a good and clear subject line
- proofreading for spelling and punctuation
- showing appreciation
- avoiding using the cc option too much (does anyone else really need to be copied?)
- being patient. Remember that your professor likely receives many email messages and might not respond within hours; you certainly should not demand a response after school hours, over weekends, or on holidays even if you think your professor is working.

TASK SIX

Answer these questions.

1. What other reasons can you think of for needing to email a professor?

2. What other reasons can you think of for visiting a professor's office hours in person?

3. Are there any items for 1 or 2 that should be on the opposite list or could be included on both lists?

4. Choose an item from the list or another item for which you think you might have to write to a professor. Draft an appropriate email message.

TASK SEVEN

Decide whether you should write an email message or schedule an office hour visit for each of these reasons. Write E for email or O for office hour.

_____ apologizing for missing class and asking for a summary of what you missed

_____ asking for a reference letter to accompany your PhD application or a job interview

_____ requesting the PowerPoint slides from the lecture

_____ asking the professor to take a quick glance at your proposal for the course research project before the due date

_____ scheduling an appointment for an office hour

_____ wondering why you earned a B instead of an A on an assignment

_____ clarifying the date of the first test (it's not on the syllabus)

_____ asking if there is a TA for the class

_____ saying you are sick and won't be in the next class

_____ inquiring about openings in the professor's research group

Reflections for TAs

1. Why might a TA visit the professor's office hours or schedule a meeting (the professor for whom the TA is working)?

2. Why might a TA email the professor rather than visiting his or her office?

3. Can students email the TA? What should a student email the TA about? What should the student visit the TA's office hours about?

4. Choose an item for which you would email the professor you are working for. Draft an appropriate email message.

2

The Structure, or Moves, of an Office Hour

Office hours actually have some structure to them. This structure is often unfamiliar to or overlooked by students, which usually becomes apparent when students visit professors in their offices. It is important (1) to be familiar with the parts, (2) to know the language—verbal and non-verbal—you should use as you progress from part to part, and (3) to use the proper etiquette throughout the interaction. According to Limberg (2007), office hours tend to progress through five phases or *moves*. The five moves are:

1. Prefacing Sequence: Summons and Answer
2. Opening
3. Outlining Academic Business
4. Negotiating Academic Business
5. Closing

Each of the five moves will be explained and discussed.

Move 1: Prefacing Sequence: Summons and Answer

Waiting To Be Invited In

Think of visiting someone's home. Even if you know that person very well, you do not usually walk in without being invited. The same is true of office hours. Any office hour visit begins with a prefacing sequence that includes the *summons* or being called or invited in and the *answer or response* to that summons. You should wait for a summons before entering the professor's office. This is especially important when there is someone else already meeting with the professor or if the professor is on the phone. You do need to make sure the professor knows you are there, especially if they are immersed in work, looking at their computers, are talking on the phone, or are meeting with someone else. How can you do this?

- Knock lightly on the door.
- Make eye contact.
- Sit in a chair or position yourself outside the office so the professor can see you and knows that you are there.
- Say *Hello* or *Hi, Professor* [Last Name] (e.g., Professor Smith).

Common Ways Professors Summon

There are several phrases professors might use to let you know they are ready for you to enter the office and begin the interaction.

> *Come in.*
>
> *Come on in.*
>
> *Were you waiting to see me?*
>
> *Sit down.*
>
> *Have a seat.*

*Notes: *Come on in* is considered less formal and friendlier than *come in*. *Come in* and *come on in* might be used together with the option to sit: *Come on in and have [or take] a seat.*

On some occasions, when you go to an office hour that is not scheduled ahead of time, you may need to get the professor's attention in order to get the summons. You might do this by offering a greeting and asking for a summons.

EXAMPLES

> *You*: Hi, Professor Williams. Do you have a minute?
>
> *Professor*: Sure. Come on in.

> *You*: Hi, Dr. Michaels. It's your office hours now, right?
>
> *Professor*: Yeah. You're in luck. Nobody's here. Come on in.

> *You*: Can I bother you for a few minutes?
>
> *Professor*: Sure. Come in. I'll be right with you. [I'll be with you in a minute.]

Non-Verbal Summons

Sometimes summons are accompanied by a non-verbal cue and sometimes there are no words—just a non-verbal cue that means "come in" or "wait." For example, professors might wave you in with their hands or they might point at the chair they want you to sit in for the meeting. These non-verbal summons might also accompany a verbal summons such as those previously mentioned. Professors may rely on these non-verbal summons if they are on the phone when you arrive. If the call is not private, they might wave you in or indicate that you should sit while they finish the call. If they are not ready for you to enter, professors might hold up their pointer finger to indicate that they just need a minute or two to finish their conversation. If this non-verbal cue is given alone, you should wait outside the office. If this non-verbal cue happens after they have waved you in or indicated that you should sit, you should do so but remain quiet until they finish the call.

Answers

After you receive the verbal or non-verbal summons, you need to respond appropriately.

- If the professor waves you in, enter.
- If the professor indicates/points to the chair, sit.
- If the professor gives a verbal summons, say "Thank you" and follow any instruction to enter and/or sit.

TASK EIGHT

Compare the prefacing sequence outlined to an office hour you have experienced. Think about any meeting you might have had with an instructor or professor, or even a person in a position of authority.

1. Do you need to wait for a summons? What kinds of summons have you seen used?

2. Are the summons listed more or less formal than what you are accustomed to?

3. Which method do you think is the best way to get the person's attention? Can you think of others to add to the list?

TASK NINE

Underline or highlight each summons you find in these office hour interactions. Circle or highlight in another color each response to the summons.

1. *Student:* May I ask a quick question?
   Professor: Sure. Sit right down.
   Student: I'll try not to take much time.

2. *Professor:* I'll be with you in a second. [Points at the chair across from his desk.]
   Student: [Sits.]
   Professor: What can I do for you?

3. *Professor:* Come on in, Ali.
   Student: Thanks.

4. *Professor:* Have a seat.
   Student: Thanks. I just have a quick question about the assignment.

5. *Student:* It's your office hours now, yes?
   Professor: Yes. I'll be right with you. Sit down.

6. *Professor:* [Waves student in.]
   Student: [Enters and sits.]

Reflections for TAs

1. Do you/Can you use the same types of summons as a professor for your office hours?

2. Do TA office hours have the same prefacing sequence as professor office hours? What is similar? What is different?

3. How do students answer a TA? Is it the same as, similar to, or different from the answers they give professors during office hours?

4. Write a role-play of a student-TA prefacing sequence.

TASK TEN

Look at this transcript from a TA office hours session. This is an example of a TA office hour that has several students attending at the same time, which is something you may encounter when you begin college. Underline or highlight any summons you find. Circle or highlight in another color any answers you find.

Student 1: Can I ask a quick question?

TA: Sure. Sit down here with me.

Student 1: Do I need to do a long calculation and show all my work for the assignment?

TA: Yeah. I think that's best. Professor Bunting is really strict about that.

[knocking on door]

Student 2: Um. Can I join the office hour?

TA: Sure. Come on in. What can I do for you?

Student 2: I don't understand if Parts A and B in the homework are the same. Do you have to figure them out the same way or use different equations?

TA: Different. Try it. I'll help someone else while you give it a try. Then I'll check your answers.

Student 3: [Standing at door.]

TA: Hey. Feel free to sit down. [Points at chair.]

Student 3: I'm wondering if you can check my answers to Problems 10 through 12.

Speaker 2: Sure thing. Come in here though so that everyone can hear my answers. I bet a lot of people have the same question. Those problems are the hardest.

Student 2: Yeah. I'd like to hear those answers.

Student 4: Can I join, too?

TA: Absolutely. Let's all move to one table and work on those last problems in the set together.

TASK ELEVEN

Answer these questions using the script in Task Ten.

1. Should there have been more or different summons? Why do you think so?

2. Should there have been more answers or different answers? Why do you think so?

3. Role-play the script with a partner and add or change the summons and responses.

Reflections for TAs

1. How is this similar to what you have experienced as a
   TA or as a student visiting a TA?

2. Do you think this was a successful TA office hour?
   Why or why not?

3. How do you or will you summon students during
   your office hours? How do you expect or hope they
   will answer?

Office hours with TAs don't always have a summons because they may be open, meaning students may come and go at different times and they may be attended by many students at the same time. In fact, they may be attended by students in other sections of the same course. Regardless, you might discover that the other students have the same question(s) or concern(s) you have.

Interrupting

Because many TA office hours are held with other students present, you may have to interrupt to get the information you came for. It is best, of course, to wait for a natural break in the conversation to ask your own questions. When you first arrive, you should enter, even without a summons, and take a seat. Listen carefully to determine which problem, question, or topic the students and TA are discussing. If you can't, raise your hand as you would in class. When you are acknowledged by the TA, either ask what the topic is (*Which question are you talking about? What problem are you on?*) or ask your own question (*Is this a good time for me to ask about Question 6? I was hoping we could talk about Problem 8*).

There are some good phrases you can use to interrupt during an office hour meeting with other students:

INTERRUPTING (AT AN APPROPRIATE TIME WHENEVER POSSIBLE)

Excuse me, but…

Sorry to interrupt, but…

Sorry to cut in.

If I could interrupt for a second…

GETTING ATTENTION (WHEN YOU ENTER AN OFFICE HOUR WITH A TA THAT IS IN PROGRESS)

Can I ask a question?

Could I say something here?

I have a question.

Keeping Your Turn (when someone new has joined the office hour and interrupted you)

Okay, but I'd just like to finish this point.

If you could wait for a second, I'm just about to finish.

Let me just finish this last point.

Continuing Your Turn (after someone has interrupted you)

Getting back to what I was saying...

As I was saying,...

In any case,...

Anyway...

TASK TWELVE

Answer these questions about interrupting.

1. How do you feel about interrupting other people who are talking? How do you feel when other people interrupt you?

2. Which of these phrases do you think are more or less direct? More or less polite? Which would you use during an office hour? Why?

Reflections for TAs

1. How is this similar to what you have experienced as a TA or as a student visiting a TA during group office hours?

2. How do you think students who interrupt too much should be managed?

3. How do you incorporate students who don't interrupt? What can you do or say to get them involved in the office hour?

Move 2: Opening

After being summoned and accepting the summons, office hours interactions usually include an opening sequence that typically has three parts:

- a greeting
- an identification (most often only used by the student and only when needed)
- small talk

Greetings

Greetings are often used by both parties—the professor and the student. Office hours are considered more formal than other interactions, especially if you are a new student or you are meeting a professor you have not met before. Therefore, the greetings tend to be more formal than informal. Despite this formality, greetings in English often sound more casual or informal. For example, *Good morning* will sound more like *G-mornin'* or *Mornin'*. Because of the expectation of formality, students should avoid casual greetings such as *Hey, What's up? What's happening?* or *What's new?*

Although office hour interactions tend to be more formal, there is some variance depending on how well you know the professor (maybe you have taken other classes with this professor), how many people are in the class (does the professor know everyone?), or how many times you have met with this professor (is this your first office hour visit?). Some common more formal greetings to use when beginning an office hour include:

Good morning. / Good afternoon.

Hi. / Hello.

How are you?

Good to see you. / Nice to see you.

TASK THIRTEEN

How would you respond to each greeting listed? Think about a formal and informal response.

Greeting	Formal Response	Informal Response
Good morning, Professor Lee.		
Hi, Dr. Dalton.		
Hello, Professor Smith.		
How are you today, Dr. Woodlawn?		
It's good to see you, [TA].		

TASK FOURTEEN

Greet five fluent or near fluent English speakers. Complete the chart with the greeting you used and the response you heard. If you are not in a location in which you can complete the chart with your own live data, watch a television show or read a script online. Complete the chart.

Greeting	Response

TASK FIFTEEN

Analyze the answers to your chart.

1. Were the responses to the greetings what you expected to hear?

2. Did you hear any other greetings and/or responses that you can use when speaking in those settings?

3. What might affect the greeting or response? In other words, do factors such as gender, status, relationship, age, time, or location/setting affect the greetings and/or the responses?

Reflections for TAs

1. How do you or will you greet students who come to your office hours?

2. Should TAs be greeted differently than professors? Why or why not?

3. In which circumstances are TAs greeted the same as or different from professors?

Identification

Unless the professor knows you very well, you should identify yourself. This is true even if you have an appointment and the professor knows you are coming. You might begin an identification in this case with something like: *Hi, Professor Dixon. We have an appointment to talk about your research.* The identification is even more important if the professor does not know you or does not know you well.

EXAMPLES

My name is Joon. I'm in your Business Essentials class on Tuesdays and Thursdays at 8:30.

I'm in your Computer Science 101 class. I'm Michael.

I'm Cecile from your Academic Writing class.

If the professor knows you, you might not have to use your name. However, even if you have an appointment, it is nice to remind the professor why you are visiting. They are likely to respond with *Of course, Yes,* or *I remember* followed by a summons such as *Come on in.*

EXAMPLES

I made an appointment with you to ask a question about the lecture from Tuesday's Business Essentials class.

I'm here to pick up my paper that you graded.

If you do not know the professor at all—for example, if you are in a large class with hundreds of students—an identification is absolutely essential.

EXAMPLES

> *My name is Robert. I'm an Electrical Engineering major and I wanted to talk to you about an article you published in an IEEE journal.*

> *We haven't met yet, but my name is Lu. My roommate, Rui, is in your research group and suggested I talk with you to see if there was a chance I could join your team.*

> *I'm a student in your Psychology 101 class. I'm here to take the quiz I missed when I was in the hospital.*

In some cultures and settings, titles or *honorifics*, such as *Mr., Ms., Professor,* or *Dr.,* are used in academic or professional settings. However, in many U.S. settings, these are not used as often. At a U.S. university, especially at the graduate level, students may even call professors by their first names. To be safe, you might want to use honorifics or titles when:

- you are meeting a professor for the first time.
- you are sending an email requesting an office hour meeting.
- you are part of a very large class.
- you have not developed any sort of working relationship with the professor.
- you want to show respect.

Remember, you know the professor, but the professor may or may not know you!

Depending on the same considerations previously listed, at some point the professor may "correct" you or let you know that it is okay to call them by their first name.

EXAMPLES

> *Student*: Hi, Professor Dodier. I'm here to ask a question about the lecture.
>
> *Professor*: Come on in. Call me Paige.

> *Student*: Hi, Dr. Lee. I'm here to pick up my Week 5 test results.
>
> *Professor*: This is our fifth meeting. Please call me William.

TASK SIXTEEN

List some common honorifics you have heard used for professors in schools or universities.

TASK SEVENTEEN

Answer these questions.

1. When do you use an honorific or title?

2. When do you use a professor's last name?

3. When do you use a professor's first name?

Reflections for TAs

1. Do TAs have any honorifics? What should students call TAs?

2. Is this the same as or different from TAs or classroom aides in high schools or international universities?

3. How do TAs address the professors they work for? Do they use honorifics? When?

Small Talk

Small talk is not usually a lengthy part of the office hour, but it does pave the way for the next stage of the office hour meeting. It is difficult to predict how much small talk there will or will not be, if there is any at all. Factors affecting small talk might be the professor's personality, the discipline or academic business to be conducted, the professor's schedule (if he or she has many meetings scheduled and needs to stay on time), or how many students the professor has in class (and how well the professor knows you). If you are one of 300 students in an introductory undergraduate class, the professor might not be as inclined to engage in a lot of small talk. However, if you are one of the professor's advisees or are in a small, upper-level course (possibly you are majoring in this field), then the professor may be more engaged because he or she will see you more than this one time. Try to pay attention and "read the cues" the professor is sending. Pay attention to the language. If the answers are very short, then the professor might not want to spend any time on small talk. There might be just one question and then he or she will move along to Move 3 very quickly.

When participating in small talk, both parties are responsible for participating. You are probably familiar with some common general small talk topics: the weather, hobbies, work, or weekend plans. These are common on campus, too.

■ weather	*I'm so tired of the rain! What about you?*
■ hobbies	*Do you like hiking? I heard there is a new hiking club on campus.*
■ work or homework	*I work in the student union.* *There is so much to do before midterms.*
■ weekend plans	*Do you have fun weekend plans?* (end of the week) *How was your weekend?* (beginning of the week)

Some small talk topics are more uniquely common on a college campus; you should be familiar enough with them in case there is a small talk exchange about these topics. Common college campus small talk topics include:

■ the football team (or other sports)	*Did you see/go to the football game Saturday?*
■ the campus newspaper	*Did you see the* Daily [student newspaper] *today?*

■ campus events	*I heard the Registrar is changing the grading scale.*
■ food or cafeterias	*I heard the new café in the engineering quad is good.*

Like any other small talk, some topics should be avoided: references to age, salary, personal characteristics (like weight), religion, or political views.

The kind of small talk that is common before moving on to the academic business (Move 3) would be asking a simple, general question:

How's your day going?

Did you have a good weekend?

What do you think about this weather we're having?

How are your classes going?

These kinds of questions often elicit short responses that make it possible to achieve Move 2 before moving on—getting to the business or purpose of the office hour meeting. Small talk questions, whether you ask them or answer them, should not lead to a long response or story.

TASK EIGHTEEN

Write a possible response to each question a professor might ask you during small talk at an office hour.

1. How's your day going?

2. Did you have a good weekend?

3. What do you think about this weather we're having?

4. How are your classes going?

TASK NINETEEN

Make a list of other small talk topics that you can use when talking to professors. Would you add any different topics for a TA? Make a second list of other small talk topics to avoid. Do a quick online search for appropriate small talk topics if you cannot think of any on your own.

Small Talk Topics to Use	Small Talk Topics to Avoid

Reflections for TAs

1. Is small talk different during a TA's office hours? How?

2. What can you/do you want to talk to about with students in your TA sessions?

3. Write a role-play in which a student and TA are participating in small talk.

Move 3: Outlining Academic Business

Consider that the first two moves (summons and greeting) might go like this:

Marco: Dr. Jones, I'm here for our meeting.

Professor: Come on in.

Marco: Thanks. I'm Marco from your Tuesday Computer Science 101 class.

Professor: Yes, I see you always sitting near the front of the room. How are things going?

Marco: Busy. I have two midterms this week, so I'm studying a lot.

Professor: It's that time of year. How can I help you today?

The last question posed here indicates that the professor does not want to engage in any more small talk and is ready to proceed. This type of statement or question leads into Move 3: Outlining or Stating the Academic Business (or the purpose). The motivation for the office hour visit must be now clarified. In this example, the professor asks for it specifically. However, the student can provide the purpose as well. While this move is only one or two statements long, they are very important statements because they let the professor know exactly why you are there.

Examples

I'm here to talk to you about my paper.

I wanted to go over my test scores with you.

I was hoping to get some more information about what you said in the lecture.

You said we could come by if we had questions.

I wanted to explain why I missed class.

You mentioned a book during your lecture today and said you had a copy in your office if we wanted to take a look.

You talked about your first job in the engineering industry today. I was hoping to hear more about your experience.

I was wondering if we could talk about my topic for my research project.

One of the other students said he got a copy of a journal article from you. Can I get a copy of that, too?

I came by to see if you could look at my essay.

Reflections for TAs

1. Give some examples of Move 3 that you might use when visiting the professor you are working for?

2. What types of motivations have you heard or do you expect students to have when they visit your TA office hours?

3. Write a short role-play in which you are meeting with the professor for whom you work. List your motivation for the visit.

Move 4: Negotiating and Resolving Academic Business

Move 4 takes the most time and is also the most varied depending on Move 3—the reason for your visit to the professor's office hours. During this step, the professor or TA and you, the student, will spend a lot of time conversing about whatever the academic business might be and constructing a solution. Among the many types of academic business are:

- editing a paper you are writing for your class
- clarifying some information from the lecture
- confirming dates or information for a test
- picking up papers, quizzes, tests, or some other type of paperwork
- going over answers

Review the reasons for office hour visits in Chapter 1 as well as Moves 1 through 3.

TASK TWENTY

As you have progressed through this book, what other reasons can you think of that you might need to use office hours for? Be specific.

Many office hour interactions will involve asking for help, asking for clarification, asking for advice, and/or making an excuse/explaining why something happened.

Asking for Help

You will need several types of language phrasing to effectively negotiate academic business. One of the most important skills to master is asking for help, which is likely the overarching reason you are attending an office hour. Sometimes it is easy to ask for help; other times it can be more challenging. Regardless, beginning your requests with a phrase that lets the professor know you are seeking help will make it clear what academic business it is you need to negotiate.

You must have reasonable expectations. There is a difference between expectation and obligation—what you expect someone to do for you may not be their responsibility or job, and they may simply have different expectations of you. Professors hold office hours and they usually want to help you—but within reason. They do not have to grant any request you make, especially if they feel it is unfair or unreasonable, such as asking them to give an extra read to your paper in advance of the due date. If you do not understand the lecture a professor gave in class, you cannot expect the professor to re-teach the whole lecture and you certainly cannot expect the professor to do that week after week. This might be a good reason to visit the TA's office hours, if available, rather than going to the professor's office hours. In any case, using polite and proper wording to ask for help is more likely to garner you the help you need. Notice the use of modals such as *could* and *would* and how the use of modals adds an element of politeness and formality.

EXAMPLES OF ASKING FOR HELP

I'm sorry to bother you, but....

Could I bother you for a minute?

Would you be willing to....

I was wondering if you could/would....

Would you mind....

I hope you don't mind, but could/would you....

If it's not too much trouble, could/would you....

I hate to impose, but I could use [some help with]....

Other more direct ways to ask for help require you toconsider how well you know the professor and what it is you are asking for help with. The bigger the imposition your request is, the less direct you should be (i.e., the more you should *hedge*). Notice that this list uses fewer introductory phrases to soften the tone and uses fewer modals. Of course, you can add *please* to any request to add an element of politeness and formality.

EXAMPLES OF DIRECT REQUESTS FOR HELP

Can you help me?

Do you think you can...?

Do you have a minute to help me with...

Can you...?

To make these phrases a little less direct, preface them with *I'm sorry, but* or *Excuse me, but.*

You should also note that direct requests may not always be in the form of a question:

I need some help with....

I don't understand the....

TASK TWENTY-ONE

Think about each of these situations. What language/phrasing would you use to ask for help?

1. You just arrived on campus and want to enroll in a professor's class. Unfortunately, you need special permission since the class is already full.

2. You want your English instructor to proofread your resume for an internship you want to apply for. This is not part of your regular English class assignment.

3. You need to meet with your advisor to choose classes for next semester, but you have no idea what courses to take.

4. You attend a TA's office hours but you still don't know how to solve the math problems because you didn't understand the lecture.

TASK TWENTY-TWO

Review the situations in Task Twenty-One. Would any of these be better served via email rather than an in-person office hour meeting? Which ones? For situations that would be better handled via email, write the email message. For situations that might be better handled during an office hour, write a dialogue that includes Moves 1–3 and Move 4 (asking for help).

Clarifying and Getting More Information

Office hours are often used to clarify or make something more clear or less confusing or to get information about lectures or assignments. There are certain words or phrases you can use to let the professor know that the academic business you want to cover is clarifying or getting more information. You can use these phrases when meeting with TAs or professors. Of course, you should be as specific as you can when you make your request.

EXAMPLES OF ASKING FOR CLARIFICATION AND GETTING MORE INFORMATION

I'm not sure I understood how to determine which equation to use. Can you explain it again?

I missed the explanation about when the election process changed. When / What was the date you said...?

I'd like a little more information on the last part of the lecture about....

Would you repeat / say again the information about...?

Can you go over that part about [X] again?

What is an example of that type of science?

Did you say that he was the inventor?

Remember that during office hours or even during class, professors and TAs will often look for evidence that you understand. Listen for these clarification requests from professors. Note that you may also hear these during class.

Do you understand? / Understand?

Are you following? / Following?

Is that clear? / Clear?

Do you see / know what I mean?

See / Know what I mean?

Does that make sense?

See what I'm saying / doing?

There are also more direct and less formal requests.

Got that?

With me so far?

Make sense?

Okay?

When you are asked for clarification, you need to respond appropriately. Do you understand or do you still need clarification or more information?

Confirm: Yes, I understand.	Clarify: No, I don't/still don't understand.
I understand.	I don't think / still don't think I understand.
I get it. / Got it.	I don't get it.
I'm good. / I'm okay.	Huh? / What?
I see what you mean / You're saying....	I'm sorry. I don't see....

As a student, you may ask if you have something right or wrong. You can always ask questions like:

Is this correct?

Is this right?

Did I do this the right way?

Professors or TAs might also simply confirm whether or not you have something correct. Tone of voice is very important here. Even if the student is wrong, professors and TAs do not want to sound demeaning or make the student feel bad. Here are some words and phrases you may hear letting you know if you are right or wrong.

Correct	Incorrect
Yes / Yep / Yeah	No / Nope
That's right.	No, that's not it.
Right.	Sorry. That's not right. Let's try again.
Exactly.	Not quite. Close. Sort of. / Kind of. Not exactly.
Correct.	Sorry, but no.
Perfect.	Not quite.
Okay.	No, that's not it. Let's try again.
You've got it.	That's still not it. Let's try again.

TASK TWENTY-THREE

Choose a chapter from a textbook you are using or from a field of study you hope to pursue when you go to college. Pretend the first page of the chapter is a lecture a professor gave in class. Write some clarification questions about the information that you could use when you visit the professor's office.

Reflections for TAs

1. How do you/can you prepare for when students visit your TA hours and ask you a clarification or getting more information question?

2. Are there any other phrases that TAs might use that professors would not? List them. Why might this be the case?

3. Write a short role-play in which a student visits your office hours and asks for more information about the course for which you are or want to be a TA. Add your answers and make sure to confirm whether the student understands or not.

VIDEO ANALYSIS TASK ONE:
Getting More Information from a Professor

Watch the video at www.press.umich.edu/elt/compsite/ officehours. Use the transcript to answer the questions.

> *Professor*: So, there's just one handout for the lecture today, um, and you know the exam's on Wednesday. Are there any questions on, about the exam? And you know the review is tonight and so you need to look over your study questions and generate the, you know, the content of the review session tonight. Ah, there's also some sample questions on the web so check that out. And I looked over the first exam and there's some stuff, um, that we've been talking about today on the exam and also some information that we went over, uh, earlier as well. Um, ok, so, any questions?
>
> *Student 1*: Um, excuse me, is the exam going to be in this building?
>
> *Professor*: Yeah. All the exams are, are in this building, and, uh, you don't need to bring any books or anything 'cause we are gonna give you the books. And, no calculators. Uh, just show your work so that we can see everything on, on the, the paper.
>
> *Student 2*: I'm sorry, did you say that today's lecture is on the exam?
>
> *Professor*: I'm sorry, what, what was your question?
>
> *Student 2:* Is today's lecture on the exam?
>
> *Professor*: Good question. I'm sorry. It is not on the exam. Okay? It will include up to last Wednesday's lecture. Good question.

Student 3: Excuse me, um. If I understood you, you said there was materials to help us on the website? Is that right?

Professor: Yes, that's right.

Student 3: Thank you.

Student 1: Um, do you have any extra worksheets?

Professor: Oh, uh, no. If you're missing worksheets or handouts, the best thing is to do is to just email me or let me know and, uh, I can try to make some more. You could also then come up to my office and look in the box outside my office. Or you could even ask somebody else. But check, um, my box anyway. Ok, so everyone is all set for Wednesday, right?

QUESTIONS

1. What language do the participants use to clarify?

2. Do the participants know if they have understood correctly? Do they get the information they were looking for?

3. At the end of the interaction, are the students satisfied? Why do you think so?

4. Do the students feel good at the end of this interaction? Why do you think so?

5. Do you think the instructor did a good job of making sure the students understood? Do you think the students are ready for the exam?

6. What do you think is most interesting about this interaction? How is this similar to or different from interactions with professors or instructors that you have had?

7. Mark the script with the different types of language you recognize from Moves 1 through 4 that were covered in this book and any moves you see. What kinds of language might have improved this discussion?

8. How is this small group meeting with professor
   the same as or different from an office hour?
   What moves are missing? Rewrite the script to
   include what is missing before, during, or after
   the content that is already there as if this were an
   office hour.

Reflections for TAs

1. What would you do the same or differently if this
   were a TA office hour?

Asking for Advice

Sometimes office hours are used to ask for academic advice—for example, what classes to take, what you can do to improve your grade, or what books you should read. Advice topics can be quite varied. For example, they may extend beyond academia: you can ask for advice about job interviews, companies, types of jobs, or job prospects. Depending on how well you know your advisor or a professor, you may also ask for more personal advice, especially if you are feeling overwhelmed or worried about things and this is affecting your work. There are certain words and phrases you should use to preface requests for advice.

EXAMPLES FOR ASKING FOR ADVICE AND/OR CONSTRUCTING A SOLUTION TO THE ACADEMIC BUSINESS

How do I...?

What do you recommend/suggest?

Do you think I should...?

What do you think would help?

What should I do about...?

Do you have any advice about...?

What do you think I should do?

Be prepared for the language professors and TAs might use in response to offer you advice.

I suggest / recommend....

You might try....

You might want to....

If I were you....

How about....

Why don't you....

You could / should....

Professors and TAs might use the imperative (command) and the *–ing* form of the verb to be more direct and stronger. Of course they might soften it by prefacing it with a phrase from the previous list. You should note, however, that even when a professor softens the phrasing, it is a command more than a simple suggestion. When someone of higher status, like your professor, suggests something, especially related to the class or your grade, it is good advice (or a command!) and you should do it. You should not visit an office hour asking for advice if you are not going to follow it.

EXAMPLE

> Imperative—*Start doing your homework earlier. Don't wait until the night before it is due.*
>
> Softened—*You might want to start doing your homework earlier. Try not to wait until the night before it is due.*
>
> Imperative—*Going to the writing center will help you learn how to edit your papers before you turn them in.*
>
> Softened—*You should consider going to the writing center to learn how to edit your papers before you turn them in.*

TASK TWENTY-FOUR

Using an asking for advice phrase, write a question you can use during an office hour.

1. You want to get a better grade.

2. You want to know the best professor for a particular course.

3. You want to find resources on campus to help you proof your papers.

4. You want to find a job after college.

5. You want to know the best books to read about a
   field of study.

6. You want to know how to improve your skills.

Reflections for TAs

1. What advice would you offer to a student for each
   question posed in Task Twenty-Four?

2. What kinds of advice might you seek from the
   professor for whom you are a TA?

3. Complete this chart with a question you imagine a
   student would ask and then write a response.

Situation	Question from Student: What is a student going to ask?	Answer to Student: What will you respond with if you are a TA?
Not understanding the problems in the homework		
Needs to know when the test is		
Missed the lecture because of illness		
Curious to know what it is like to be a TA		
Wondering the best way to prepare for graduate school		

Making Excuses

One type of language you may need during Move 4 is how to make an excuse or explain why something happened. For example, you may want to explain why you missed class, why an assignment is late, or why you do not understand something. Note that you can also use some of this language in email messages. Sometimes professors expect a very good excuse for missing a class or an assignment. The definition of "good" depends on the professor or even department or university rules. Some departments, programs, or professors may even expect doctor's notes or official word from a dean or another office, such as the vice-provost for undergraduate education.

Excuses are usually prefaced with the words *I'm sorry* or *Sorry* followed by the reason or excuse to explain why you are apologizing.

EXAMPLES

I'm sorry I missed class. I was sick so I went to the health center. I didn't expect the appointment to take so long.

Sorry I was late to class. My car broke down on the way to campus. So, I missed the date of the test you announced at the beginning of class.

TASK TWENTY-FIVE

For each situation listed, think of a good reason or excuse. What would you say if you were a student? Make sure to think of an excuse that you feel would be accepted by a professor.

1. Being late to class:

2. Turning in an assignment late:

3. Missing class:

4. Oversleeping:

5. Not understanding the class content:

6. Forgetting to bring the textbook:

7. Making a lot of mistakes:

8. Requesting an extension for an assignment:

Reflections for TAs

1. What excuses do you think you would give a professor for why you might need to cancel the office hours you need to have for his or her class?

2. Are excuses more, less, or just as important coming from a student to a TA as when they come from a student to a professor? Why do you think so?

3. What excuses do you think are good for each situation listed in Task Twenty-Five?

Responses to Excuses/Explanations

As part of Move 4, professors and TAs will respond to excuses or reasons. One likely response will be one of sympathy, especially if the excuse is very serious or excused by the university. In response to excuses or reasons, the professor or TA may offer their sympathy.

EXPRESSIONS OF SYMPATHY

I'm sorry [to hear that].

I understand.

Responses at the Conclusion of Academic Business

The professor or TA may offer congratulations at the conclusion of academic business or when you accomplished something they were teaching or explaining. For example, if you did well on the assignment or now understand the problem set, you need to complete for class, you will receive some sort of acknowledgment.

EXAMPLES

Congratulations.

Well done.

Way to go.

You got it!

Great / Good job.

You should be prepared for neither sympathy nor congratulations. Rather than an expression of sympathy, professors might simply say something like *Thanks for letting me know*. Rather than a congratulations, professors might only say *That's it* or *You can take it from here*. You should not be frustrated by this. Responses may vary based on personality, relationship (how well this professor knows you), or even the field of study.

TASK TWENTY-SIX

Think of any academic situations or excuses for which you have heard an expression of sympathy. List the situations and the expressions of sympathy you heard.

Think of any academic situations or excuses for which you have heard an expression of congratulations. List the situations and the expressions of congratulations you heard.

Reflections for TAs

1. What expressions of sympathy or congratulations do you think you would give a student during your office hours? Are these similar to or different from what you would expect the professor to say?

2. In what situations would you expect to hear these from the professor for whom you TA?

Move 5: Closing

Once academic business has been handled, it is time for you to leave the office hour. A few things typically happen as the office hour meeting concludes:

- reviewing the solution (optional)
- asking for / scheduling future meetings (optional)
- thanking or expressing gratitude (obligatory)
- leave-taking (obligatory)

Reviewing the Solution

You may or may not want to review the solution or topics you have just discussed. The professor may review the solution, but the student can also review it. Since it is you that needs to understand, you should feel comfortable enough to do this and know the language to use.

EXAMPLES

Professor: So, you're going to rewrite the introduction and resubmit it to me.

vs.

Student: So, I'm going to / I will rewrite the introduction and resubmit it to you.

Professor: You'll do the problems on page 360 and then visit the TA's office hours next week.

vs.

Student: My plan is to follow your advice. I'll do the problems on page 360. And I'll go to the TA's office hours next week.

Scheduling Another Meeting

Another part of the leaving that may or may not happen is scheduling another meeting. Again, the TA or professor might suggest another meeting or leave the possibility open, letting you know you are welcome to come back. But, it's also possible for the student to suggest or request another meeting.

FROM THE PROFESSOR

Let me know if you want to meet again.

My door is always open.

Why don't we revisit this again next week?

Let me know how it goes.

FROM THE STUDENT

I'm going to give this a try. Can I schedule another meeting if I still have trouble?

I'll stop by again and let you know how things are going.

I'll schedule another meeting if I'm still having trouble.

Is it okay with you if I schedule another meeting?

Thanking/Expressing Gratitude

Two of the four parts of Move 5 are obligatory or required. One that is required is thanking the professors and TAs for their time. This is true in email messages as well. The most common way to express thanks is simply to say *Thank you* or *Thanks*.

EXAMPLES OF OTHER PHRASES

I really appreciate the help.

I couldn't have done this without you.

You're a lifesaver.

I don't know how to thank you.

Thanks [so much] / [a lot] / [a million].

Thanks for your time.

Thank you for meeting with me.

Naturally, any expression of thanks will be followed by a response. Most people are taught that *You're welcome* or *My pleasure* are the typical responses, but these are formal. Because some professors may be more formal during office hours, you might hear these phrases. However, professors or TAs who are less formal will use other phrases.

EXAMPLES OF LESS FORMAL RESPONSES TO *THANKS*

No problem.

You bet.

Happy to help.

Don't mention it.

It was nothing.

No worries.

You got it.

TASK TWENTY-SEVEN

Answer the questions.

1. What are some of the different phrases/words you have used to thank an instructor or professor for something?

2. What other phrases/words do you use to express gratitude? How do you respond when someone thanks you for something?

TASK TWENTY-EIGHT

Offer five people some help or advice. Complete the chart with
the help or advice you used and the response you heard. If you
are not in a location in which you can complete the chart with
your own live data, watch a television show or read a script online.
Complete the chart.

Offer or Advice	Expression of Thanks

TASK TWENTY-NINE

Analyze the answers from your chart.

1. Were the responses to the offers and advice what you expected to hear?

2. Did you hear any other expressions of thanks and/or responses that you can use during office hours?

3. What might affect the response? In other words, do factors such as gender, status, relationship, age, time, or location/setting affect the greetings and/or the responses?

Reflections for TAs

1. How do you or will you respond when a student thanks you for something?

2. How do you or would you thank the professor for whom you work when they offer you advice about your TA class?

3. Do you think students thank TAs differently than they thank professors? Can you think of any phrases you would hear in a TA office hour that you don't expect you would hear in an office hour with the professor?

Leave-Taking

It is important to recognize when it is time to leave the office hour. Sometimes the TA or professor will give an indication that the meeting is over. Pay attention to those cues! Listen for the pre-goodbyes or notice when someone else is waiting. Look for non-verbal cues like the professor looking at the clock or their watch. It's also possible for the student to end the office hour. The important thing is to recognize the pre-goodbye and then the goodbye. After that, leave.

PRE-GOODBYES

It's been nice talking with you.

It was good to see you.

I have another class / student in a few minutes.

I have to get going.

GOODBYES

See you in class.

See you soon.

Bye.

Have a good day / night.

Talk to you later.

EXAMPLE DIALOGUE

Expression of Thanks: *Thanks for helping me figure out those problems.*

Response: *Glad I could help.*

Pre-Goodbye from Student: *I've gotta run. I have a class in 10 minutes.*

Pre-Goodbye from TA: *Sounds good.*

Goodbye from Student: *See you in class.*

Goodbye from TA: *See you there.*

Expression of Thanks: *Thanks for clarifying that information for me, Dr. Kurtz.*

Response: *You're welcome. Let me know if you have other questions.*

Pre-Goodbye from Professor: *But, I do have another student coming soon.*

Pre-Goodbye from Student: *Oh, I understand. I'll get out of your way.*

Goodbye from Professor: *See you in class.*

Goodbye from Student: *Bye.*

TASK THIRTY

List some other cues that could be used to indicate the meeting is over and someone should leave.

Verbal:

Non-Verbal:

Other: (example: another student waiting outside the door)

Types of Non-Verbal Communication

Non-verbal communication is extremely important in campus interactions, but especially in helping you understand the different parts or moves of an office hour interaction. What is the professor/TA doing to help you recognize the cues?

However, some non-verbal language can be interpreted negatively (for example, rolling your eyes when you disagree with someone or slumping in your seat, which looks like you are bored or not interested), so be careful.

Gestures

When you use gestures, you use parts of your body, such as hands, arms, or shoulders in place of or in conjunction with your verbal communication.

Type of Gesture	Common Message Conveyed
Shrugging your shoulders	I don't know.
Thumbs up	It's good.
Thumbs down	It's bad.
Crossing your fingers	Good luck.
Pointing	Calling attention to something or someone
Holding up your hand (palm out)	Stop.
Nodding	Yes
Shaking your head	No
High five	Congratulations!
Thumb and forefinger connected in a circle with the other fingers straight.	Okay.
Slouching	Boredom
Sitting up straight	Paying attention

Facial Expressions

Noticing facial expressions is another way to enhance communication. Two of the most common expressions of emotion are happiness (smiling) and sadness (frowning). Others that might be useful to recognize during an office hour interaction are surprise, fear, frustration, or anger.

Facial Expression	Physical Signs
Happiness	Smiling (mouth corners raised)
Sadness	Frowning (mouth corners lowered)
Surprise	Rounded mouth (mouth open, jaw dropped) Eyebrows raised
Fear	Slightly rounded mouth Eyebrows raised
Frustration	Upper lip raised Wrinkled forehead or nose
Anger	Closed mouth (lips in straight line) Eyebrows lowered

Eye Contact

Eye contact in some cultures, such as U.S. culture, is very important. What constitutes as eye contact? Eye contact is when two people look into each other's eyes at the same time. Looking into the other person's eyes is generally a sign of respect and enhances the interaction. It shows you are paying attention, but it also helps you better convey your own meanings and understand the other person because you can see their facial expressions and lip movements. Eye contact can be challenging, especially if you are from a culture in which it is considered respectful to *not* make eye contact with people who have a higher status. It might also be a challenge if students are from Asian cultures in which children are sometimes taught to look below the person's eyes as a sign of respect for that person's role, such as that of an instructor or boss.

TASK THIRTY-ONE

Practice each of the types of non-verbal communication. Then write a few notes about which ones are easiest to understand, which ones are more challenging to understand, which ones you think are most important, and which ones you most want to improve?

Reflections for TAs

1. Do you or will you use non-verbal communication when you have TA office hours?

2. Which types of non-verbal communication do you think are most important to use during office hours?

3. In which circumstances might non-verbal communication be different from that of a professor?

Pronunciation Notes

Pronunciation is another important part of communicating and interacting on campus so it plays a role in office hours interactions. Here are some pronunciation features you should be familiar with and consider when you interact with other students, TAs, or professors.

Emphasis or Stress

Emphasize or give prominence to certain syllables in a word or a certain word in a sentence. This helps your listeners understand the word or what you feel is the most important word in a statement. The word you stress can dramatically change the meaning of a sentence.

Compare these statements (capital letters indicate stress).

I didn't say that! (Someone else said that.)

I DIDN'T say that! (I deny saying that.)

I didn't SAY that! (But maybe I thought it.)

I didn't say THAT! (But I did say something else.)

Pitch

Your voice should rise and fall when you speak.

If you use a higher pitch, the statement is usually positive.

We're having a guest lecturer on Tuesday. (↑)

If you use a lower pitch, the statement is usually negative.

There are no extensions for the homework assignment. ($\downarrow$)

Tone

Tone expresses a speaker's attitude and conveys meaning behind the word choice. Even if you say the "right" words, if your tone is negative, it could hurt the interaction. Look at the example. Someone can be very happy about the lecture being canceled; someone else might be disappointed about it being canceled.

The lecture will be canceled on Friday.

TASK THIRTY-TWO

For each of these statements you might say during an office hour, say them using different stresses, pitches, and tones. Which way communicates your intent?

I'm sorry I missed class. I couldn't get any other doctor appointment.

Can you offer me some advice about which journals I should read?

What types of job opportunities are there for someone with a degree in electrical engineering?

I'm here to talk about the homework assignment.

I didn't hear what you said about the test in class.

Reflections for TAs

Think of things you have said many times or expect you'll have to say during TA office hours. Practice saying them with the appropriate stress, pitch, and tone.

VIDEO ANALYSIS TASK TWO:
Asking Questions about a Class Project:
Two Students and a Professor

Watch the video at www.press.umich.edu/elt/compsite/
officehours. Use the script to answer the questions.

Student 1: Professor? Could you explain the project a
bit more?

Student 2: Yes, that would be very helpful.

Instructor: Sure, I'd be happy to stick around and
answer a few questions. This project is a big part of
your final grade.

Student 1: Well, I know we're supposed to choose an
earthquake from history, write about its effects on
the Earth, and then make a presentation to the class.
And there's something about "interesting facts." Is
that right?

Instructor: That's right. You want to pick out some
information relevant to your specific quake,
something that the class will find interesting and
talk about that in your paper. Is that clear?

Students 1 and 2: Yes.

Student 1: How long is the paper supposed to be?

Instructor: Believe it or not, there are no length
requirements. Of course, it depends the earthquake
that you pick, so you don't need to pick a minor
quake.

Student 1: Darn! [laughing]. I do like it when I know
how many pages I have to write though.

Instructor: Well, I want you to write without worrying about how long or short it is. Once you pick your earthquake, then you can talk about any part of it, and don't worry about the, um, length. Of course, geology is important, so you want to talk about what is going on at the crust level. You might also want to add some specific facts about the epicenter and the damages that were done or were not done, and why. Got it?

Student 2: Yes. Makes sense. You want us to pick some facts we find interesting about earthquakes. Some of them can even be our opinions, right? You really can't get that wrong.

Instructor: That's right. Um. Just, you want you to say about why you find this earthquake interesting, and then I'm sure the class will agree that those same things are interesting to them. You want to cover the geological processes that we've learned about so far this term as well.

Student 1: Okay. Got it. Focus, focus on the damages and what we might learn for the future.

Instructor: Yes, that's a good start.

Student 2: Ok, and do we have to document our sources? And, if so, which style?

Instructor: MLA.

Student 1: Oh, I'm good. I've got that in my English handbook.

Instructor: Ok, that's the end of the questions. I have to run to my next class. Please feel free to email me if you have any other questions. And, good luck.

QUESTIONS

1. What language do the participants use to clarify their understanding?

2. Do the participants know if they have understood correctly? Do they get the information they were looking for?

3. At the end of the interaction, are the students satisfied? Why do you think so?

4. Does the students feel good at the end of this interaction? Why do you think so?

5. What do you think of their tone of voice?

6. What non-verbal cues are used?

7. Do you think the instructor did a good job of making sure the student understood? Do you think the students are ready for the exam?

8. What do you think is most interesting about this interaction? How is this similar to or different from office hour or professor interactions you have had?

9. Mark the script with the different types of language you recognize and any moves you see.

10. How is this small group meeting with the TA or professor the same as or different from an office hour? What moves are missing? Rewrite the script to include what is missing before, during, or after the content that is already there.

3

Do's and Don'ts of Office Hours

The last section of this book includes two videos with sample office hour meetings. Before watching the videos and analyzing the scripts, read this list of things to keep in mind when you go to office hours with a TA or professor.

Do

- Be prepared.
- Talk.
- Be honest.
- Go as often as you need to.
- Ask for an appointment if you have class during the office hours.
- Be prompt.
- Go alone (to meet a professor; you can sometimes go with friends to a TA session).

- Wait to be summoned before entering.
- Let them know why you're there.
- Use proper phrasing.

DON'T

- Be silent.
- Complain.
- Attack or lay blame.
- Make bad excuses.
- Be afraid.
- Miss an appointment without notice.
- Wait until the last minute.
- Talk over your professor or TA.
- Stay too long.
- Pretend to understand when you don't.

4

Office Hours Capstone Video Analysis Tasks

Capstone Task 1: Clarifying an Assignment During an Office Hour

Before watching the videos, be very aware that not all interactions will prescribe exactly to all five moves. And that's okay! While the elements are usually there in some form, they may not be in the same order. Or, there might be a reason for why something is not included. For example, maybe there is no pre-goodbye because you think they're in a rush. Or, maybe there is no identification because the professor and student know each other well. Think critically as you complete the analysis.

Watch the video at www.press.umich.edu/elt/compsite/officehours. Use the transcript to answer the questions.

> *Student*: Hi, Professor Montgomery. Do you have a minute?
>
> *Professor:* Yes, come on in. I have a little time before I have to leave for class. What can I do for you?
>
> *Student*: Well, I wanted to make sure that I understand the assignment for our class.

Professor: Well, It's a big part of your final grade, so I'm glad you're asking. What questions do you have?

Student: Well, I know we're supposed to do a presentation about a city or region's response to a major earthquake, um . . . Is that right?

Professor: Yes, that's right. Think about the impacts, both large and small. Both immediate and after some time. Is that clear?

Student: Yeah, but I'm just not sure I can think of enough things that have changed. Do you mean just in terms of safety?

Professor: Yes. But, my suggestion is that you think about earthquakes that aren't so recent so that you have more content—you know, more time has passed so there are more impacts. Do you know what I mean?

Student: Okay. Yeah, that helps. And there are some earthquakes we can't pick, right?

Professor: Yes, didn't the TA cover that? I thought he had a list.

Student: No, he said he didn't know there were any that were off limits.

Professor: Hold on while I give him a quick call and leave him a message. [Professor picks up phone, dials, and then leaves this voice mail message: Hi, Sung-min, this is Professor Montgomery. I'm calling because I've got a student in my office from Earth Science 101 who does not have the list of earthquakes that should not be used for the assignment. I wanted to let you know that I sent that to you in an email a few weeks ago. Can you let the students know what those are? Let me know if you have questions. Thanks. Bye. [Professor hangs up.] Okay . . . well, you heard that. So, you'll be getting that and that should clear things up, right?

Student: Right. Thank you. Um, and one other thing I'm wondering about is how personal we should make our presentation.

Professor: Can you explain what you mean a bit more?

Student: Well, ah, I was thinking about maybe using personal stories or quotations from somebody who has actually survived the earthquake that I pick.

Professor: Well, it's a good idea, but, more than anything else, your presentation has to cover what happened afterward.

Student: Ok. Um, the reason I was asking is because I actually know some people who were at the World Series game in California when the earthquake struck.

Professor: Well, as a matter of fact, I was in Oakland a few days before that one hit and, oddly enough, I was even driving over that bridge—you know the one that collapsed during the quake.

Student: Wow. That's kinda scary to think about.

Professor: It is. It is. And I do think about that a lot. Do you have any more questions?

Student: Ah, just one more thing. Ah, if I do use quotes or interview someone, and I decide to use that in my paper, I'm not really sure I know how to document it. Um. What I mean is, if these quotations are not from a published source, how do I include it? I just have stories my grandpa told me. See what I mean?

Professor: Well, this department uses APA, and I'm pretty sure that the reference manuals or the online resources will give you that type of example—an interview or personal communication. Okay?

Student: Ok, thank you. I'll check my English handbook then.

Professor: Is there anything else?

Student: No, I'm good. Thank you.

Professor: Sure.

QUESTIONS

1. What clarification phrases were used?

2. How does the student let the professor know she understands?

3. Did the student really understand the assignment? Why do you think so?

4. Does the instructor give the student enough time to ask for clarification? Support your answer.

5. What do you think of the speakers' tone of voice?

6. What non-verbal cues are used?

7. Do you think the instructor did a good job of making sure the student understood?

8. What do you think is most interesting about this interaction? How is this similar to or different from office hour interactions you have had?

9. Mark the script with the different types of language you identify and the moves the speakers use before answering these questions.

   a. What do you think of the student asking for a summons before waiting for the professor to summon her?

   b. How do you feel about the greeting and identification in this video? Was there any small talk? Why or why not?

    c. What part of Move 3 did the student use? Do you feel it was appropriate?

    d. What types of language from Move 4 did you identify in the video?

    e. How does this video follow or not follow Move 5? Are reviewing the solution, scheduling another meeting, expressing thanks, and leave-taking included?

10. What do you think about the moves or lack therof in this interaction? Could the interaction have gone better or worse in terms of language or moves? Rewrite the script as you want to make it a better interaction. Include additional language from Move 4 or from other moves studied in this book.

Capstone 2: Discussing a Presentation During an Office Hour

Watch the video at www.press.umich.edu/elt/compsite/officehours. Use the transcript to answer the questions.

Student: I wanted to talk to you about the presentation for class. I'm in your 11:00 Linguistics class.

Professor: Yeah, I have a couple of minutes before I need to go to class. What's up?

Student: Well, the presentation is supposed to be about 10 minutes long, right? I'm not sure I have enough information for a presentation that long.

Professor: Well, ya, you want to keep in mind that content is the most important aspect of this. Uh, yes, 10 minutes is the goal, but really it's all about the content. Can you remind me what your topic is?

Student: Yeah. I wanted to learn about language acquisition. So, my research question is: Do we learn our second language the same way we learn our first?

Professor: Mmhmm. And, you've done the research right?

Student: Yeah. For example, I have lots of facts and figures from secondary sources—two books, two articles, um, several reliable websites. I even did some interviews with experts and conducted a survey of students who speak a second language to see what their opinions were and then I put, uh, those results in, well, I drew some conclusions of those results and put them in a PowerPoint. But when I rehearse it all, it takes about four minutes, so . . . .

Professor: Wow. Sounds like you have enough research though, right?

Student: Yeah. I think so.

Professor: So, let's think about other ways that we might be able to beef this up. Um. Let me explain. One critical thing to make sure you're doing is giving explanations. In other words, you don't want to just give facts and figures and you know show some pretty numbers. You really want to explain what those results mean. What, what do the numbers actually tell us? So, imagine that your audience is sitting there just imag, thinking: What does it mean? What does that mean for me? Uh, really try to explain why those re, results are important.

Student: Okay. I got that. Um, I'll add some more to those sections. Do you have other ideas?

Professor: Yeah, I would say another really important thing is to give examples.

Student: Okay. Um, also, I'm not sure I have a good beginning. How should I start my presentation?

Professor: Yeah, there's so many different ways you can start a presentation. Some people like to use quotations. Sometimes you can use some really interesting fact or figure just to kind of surprise everybody. You could use an anecdote, you know, tell a story that is from your own experience as a second language learner. Um, and you've certainly got a lot of experience that you can draw from. And, keep in mind too that the other students in the class are language learners as well. The university has a requirement to learn a second language, so they have a lot of experience.

Student: That's a good idea. Do you think that's a good idea for a hook?

Professor: Yeah, that I think could work. You could also consider using some interesting quotation from the people that you've interviewed. Uh, you've certainly got a lot of material to draw from. If you're going to use a quote from someone that you spoke with, uh, make sure you tell us a little about that person though, what their first language is. Uh, I think anytime you can give us a little bit more background about your, uh, the people that you've interviewed that would be really helpful. So, I think we'd be interested in knowing whether they're Spanish speakers, Arabic speakers, Mandarin speakers . . .that kind of thing.

Student: Good idea. I still have the original surveys that everyone filled out, so I could easily take pieces of, you know, quotations from, um, my surveys and I think that that would offset the concrete numbers really nicely. And, I, you know, I found some interesting trends in the survey, so . . . .

Professor: Really, what what did you find?

Student: Um, well, most of the Arabic speakers answered about the same way as the French speakers.

Professor: Wow. That's really interesting. So, I think that's something that the audience would want to hear. 'Cause you always want to think about what is what is the audience interested in. It's not just what do I have to tell people, but what is the audience really, really interested in. And again I come back to my earlier point that they're all second language learners, and so you really want to connect with them in that way.

Student: So, I should think about, um, you know everybody in class, like what they're interested in?

Professor: Yeah. Absolutely. And I think I think we've got a lot of interesting people in the class who have ideas about second language learning that are similar to yours. They have, uh, goals that may be similar or different, um, to, to yours. So, what do you know about people in the class?

Student: Well, me, for instance, I know we're all second language learners, but I want to be a second language teacher. Uh, but others in class don't. We all have different ideas for what kind of jobs we want. I know some people want to be translators. Some people want to be interpreters. Joe, uh, for instance wants to be, um, he wants to work in the government in intelligence.

Professor: Wow, I would bear that in mind. I, I think that's really important to give that kind, to consider that kind of background, um, since you have it, um, you want to use that in the presentation. Definitely.

Student: Okay. I will do that.

Professor: Um, have you given any thought to how you might end the presentation?

Student: Uh. I hadn't thought about that yet, really.

Professor: Yeah. Um. That's often really a hard part of the presentation. We often worry so much about how the beginning is going to go that we forget about how we're going to end and we don't want to just say, "Well that's it." So I would say you know keep in mind what some of the larger implications are about the research that you've done, how that might relate to the audience. You might even consider throwing a question out to the audience. For example, throwing a question out can lead into the Q & A. That might be really good.

Student: Yeah. That's good. Thanks. Okay. I think I'm going to have to work on my PowerPoint a bit more, um, before I'm ready to present. Definitely.

Professor: Yeah. Also, think about giving us a reference slide. I think it's really important just to show the fact that you've used a lot of different references in your presentation. Uh, for the references I'm not so worried whether I can read them, um, I just need to see that they're there. But that makes me think of one more really important thing. And that is your slides should complement what you say. So in other words what I'm saying is you don't want the slides to say exactly the same thing as you're going to say. I know how to read and if I can read it on the slide, I don't need to listen to you. So it's important that what you say complements what's on the slide and what's on the slide complements then, uh, what you have to say.

Student: Okay, so most of the ideas we've talked about should just be in my notes. Like, uh, you know a story to tell or example to give when each slide is actually being presented. [Instructor: Mmhmm.] And not have it written on the slide. Right?

Professor: Yes. [Student: Okay.] Exactly. Yeah. Um. You know I have have to run to class, but I think you've got enough to go on. I think you've got some food for thought, um, and you know where to go next, but I'm I'm really sorry I do need to run. Okay?

Student: Okay. Thank you so much for your help. See you in class.

Professor: Yeah. Sure thing. Bye-bye.

QUESTIONS

1. What language does the professor use to stress her main points? What words does she stress? How is her tone and pitch?

2. Is the professor enjoying this student's visit? Why do you think so?

3. At the end of the office hour, is the student satisfied? Why do you think so?

4. Does the student feel good at the end of this interaction? Why do you think so?

5. What do you think of their tone of voice?

6. What non-verbal cues are used?

7. Do you think the instructor did a good job of making sure the student understood?

8. What do you think is most interesting about this interaction? How is this similar to or different from office hour interactions you have had?

9. Mark the script with the different types of language you identify and the moves the speakers use before answering these questions.

   a. How does the prefacing sequence (Move 1) follow and not follow the prescribed order?

   b. How do you feel about the greeting and identification in this video? Was there any small talk? Why or why not?

   c. What was the Move 3 the student used? Do you feel it was appropriate?

   d. What types of language from Move 4 did you identify in the video?

e. How does this video follow or not follow Move 5? Are reviewing the solution, scheduling another meeting, expressing thanks, and leave-taking included?

10. What do you think about the moves or lack thereof in this interaction? Could the interaction have gone better or worse in terms of language or moves? Rewrite the script as you want to make it a better interaction. Include additional language from Move 4 or from other moves studied in this book.

REFERENCES

Feak, Christine B. (2013). ESP and speaking. In Paltridge, B., & Starfield, S. (Eds.), *The handbook of english for specific purposes* (pp. 35–53). New York: John Wiley & Sons, Inc.

Folse, K., & R. B. Lockwood. (2016). *4 point listening for academic purposes*. Ann Arbor: University of Michigan Press.

Limberg, H. (2007). Discourse structure of academic talk in university office hour interactions. *Discourse Studies, 9*, 176–193.

Lockwood, R. B. (2018). *Speaking in social contexts: communication for life and study in the U.S.* Ann Arbor: University of Michigan Press.

Lockwood, R. B., & K. Sippell. (2016). *4 point reading for academic purposes*. Ann Arbor: University of Michigan Press.